Christmas Favorites
❧ FOR ACCORDION ❧

ARRANGED BY
GARY MEISNER

ISBN 978-1-4234-1433-9

HAL•LEONARD®
CORPORATION
7777 W. BLUEMOUND RD. P.O. BOX 13819 MILWAUKEE, WI 53213

Visit Hal Leonard Online at
www.halleonard.com

CONTENTS

CHRISTMAS IS

Lyrics by SPENCE MAXWELL
Music by PERCY FAITH

THE CHRISTMAS SONG
(Chestnuts Roasting on an Open Fire)

Music and Lyric by MEL TORME
and ROBERT WELLS

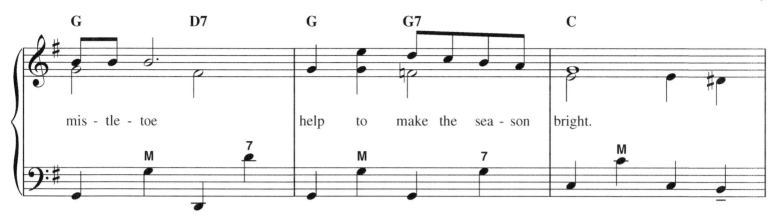

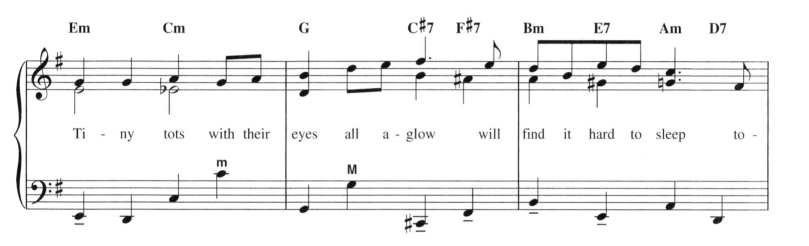

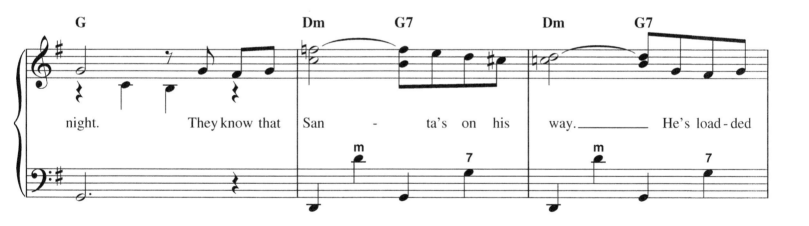

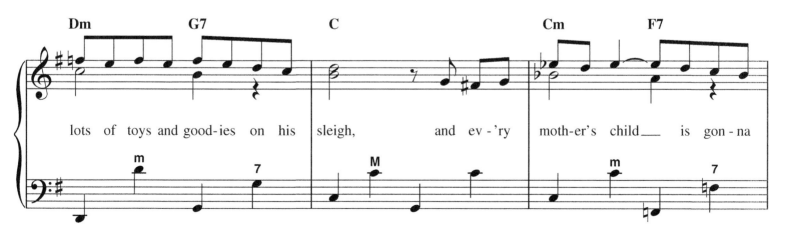

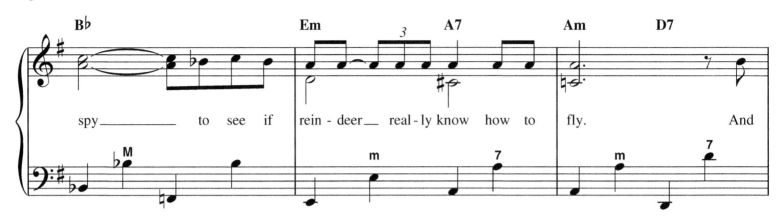

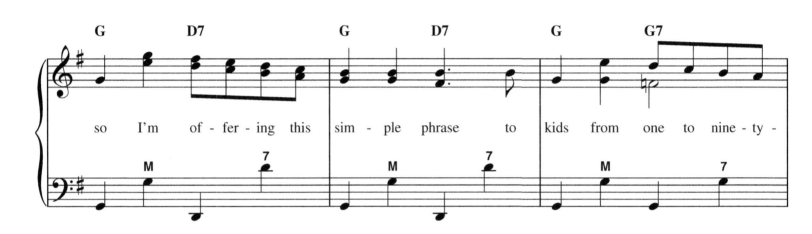

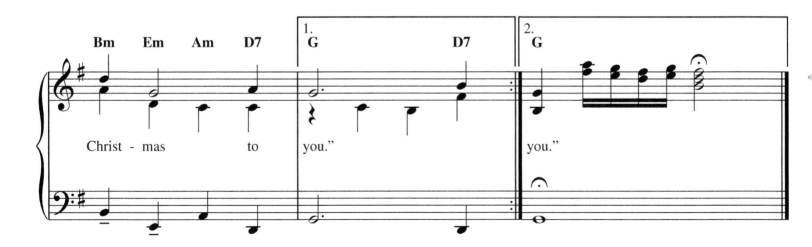

CHRISTMAS TIME IS HERE
from A CHARLIE BROWN CHRISTMAS

Words by LEE MENDELSON
Music by VINCE GUARALDI

Christ - mas time is here, hap - pi - ness and
Snow - flakes in the air, car - ols ev - 'ry -

cheer. Fun for all that chil - dren call their
where. Old - en times and an - cient rhymes of

fa - v'rite time of year.
love and dreams to share.

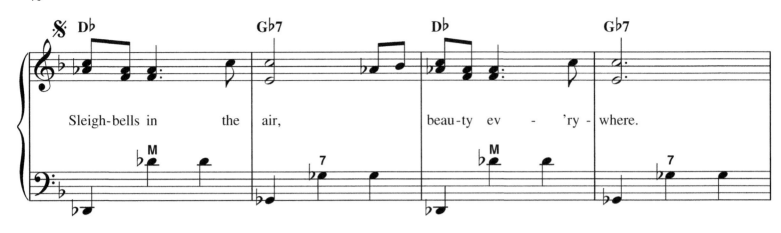

Sleigh-bells in the air, beau-ty ev - 'ry - where.

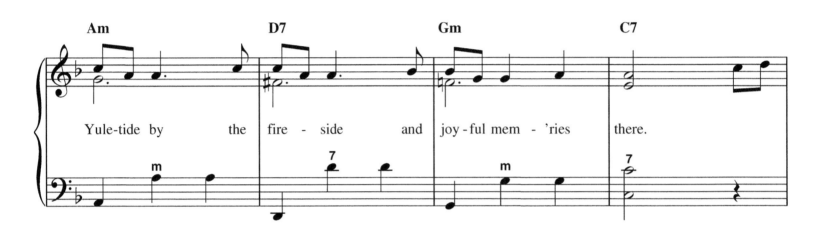

Yule-tide by the fire - side and joy-ful mem - 'ries there.

Christ-mas time is here, we'll be draw - ing near.

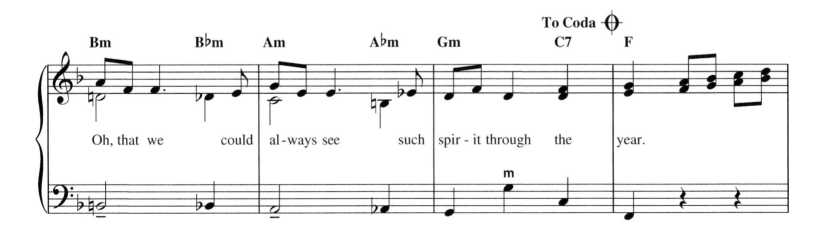

Oh, that we could al-ways see such spir - it through the year.

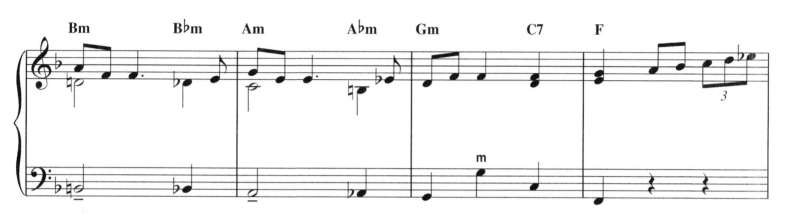

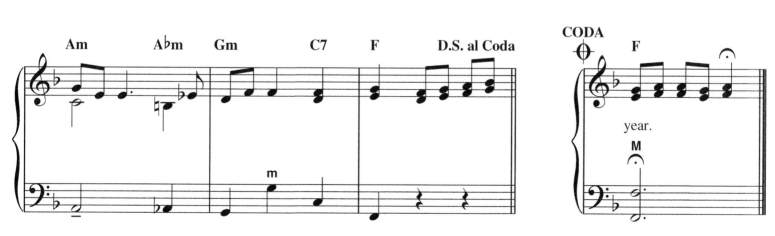

FELIZ NAVIDAD

Words and Music by
JOSÉ FELICIANO

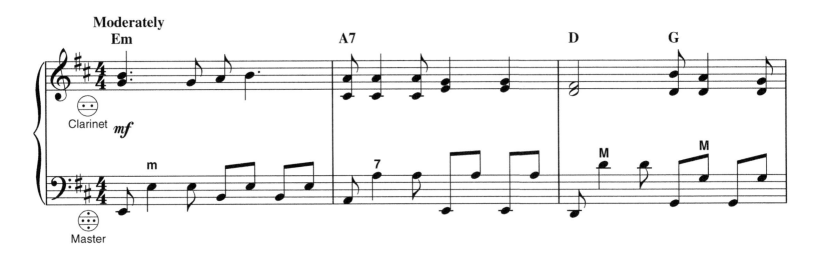

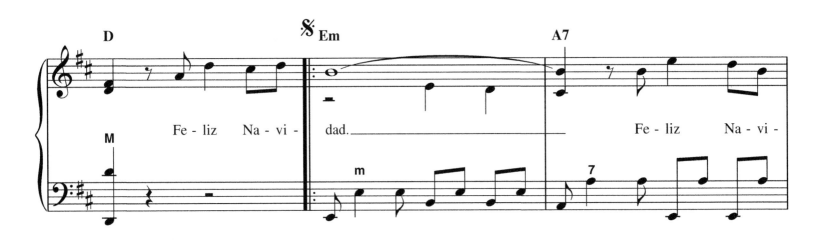

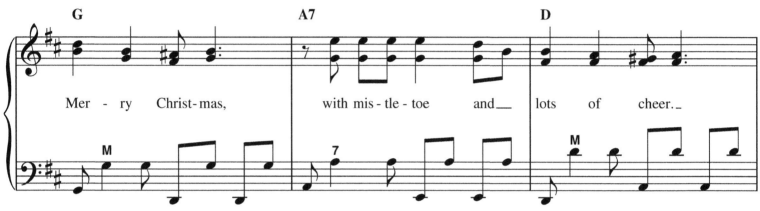

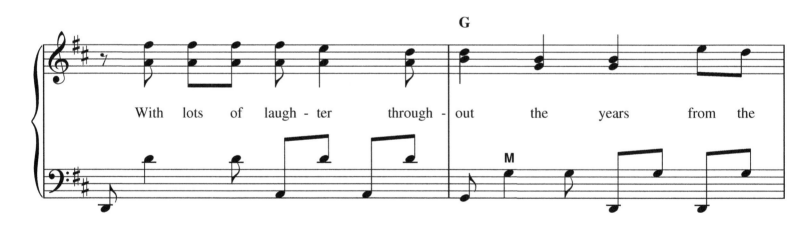

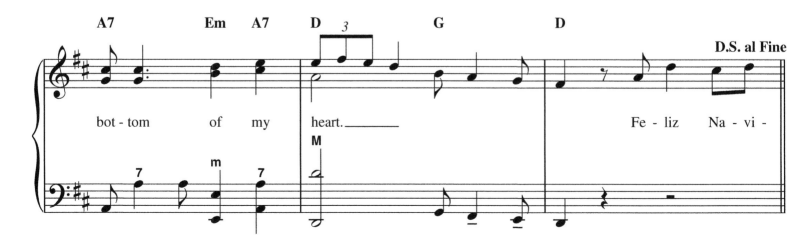

HAPPY HOLIDAY
from the Motion Picture Irving Berlin's HOLIDAY INN

Words and Music by
IRVING BERLIN

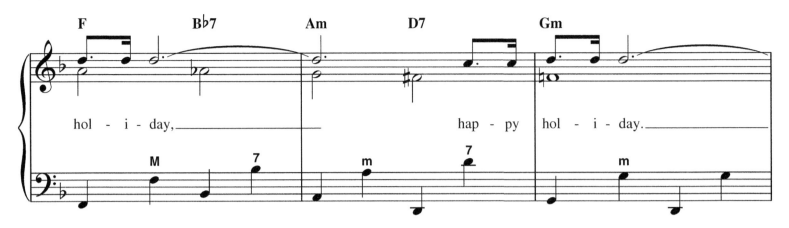

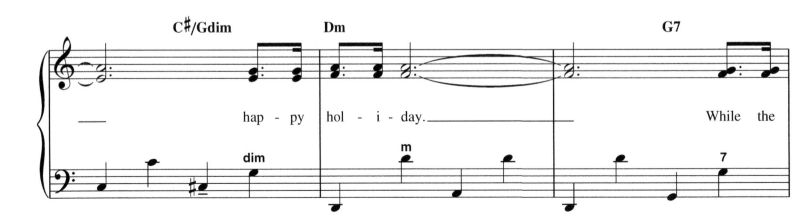

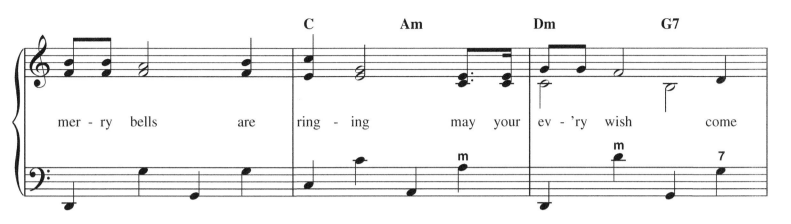

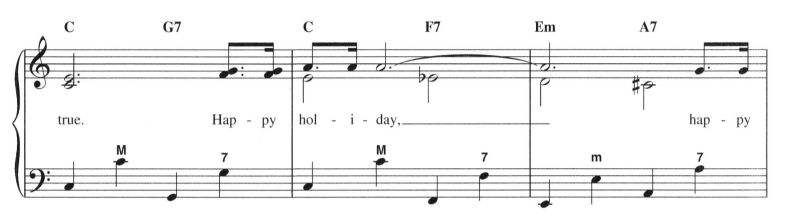

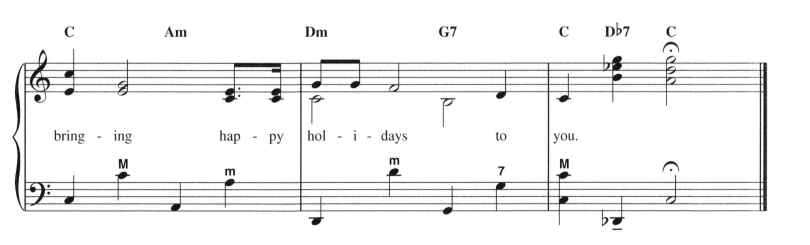

HE

Words by RICHARD MULLEN
Music by JACK RICHARDS

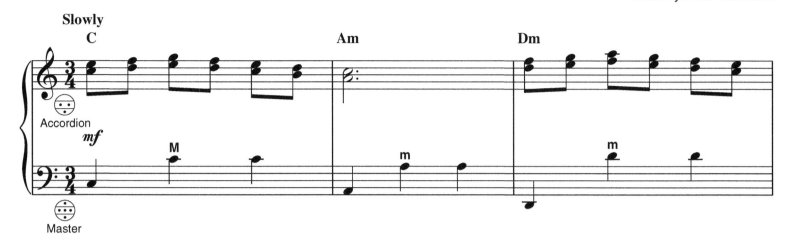

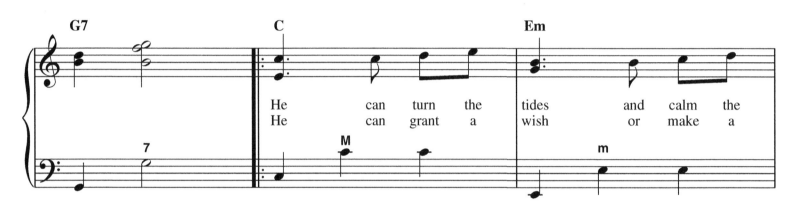

He can turn the tides and calm the
He can grant a wish or make a

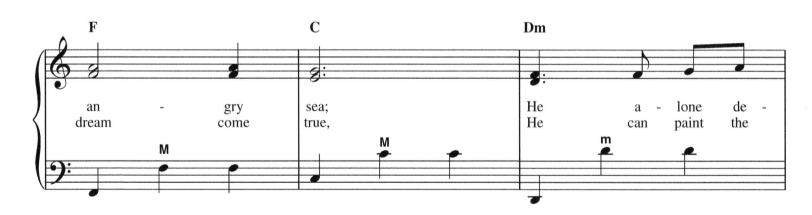

an - gry sea;
dream come true,

He a - lone de
He can paint the

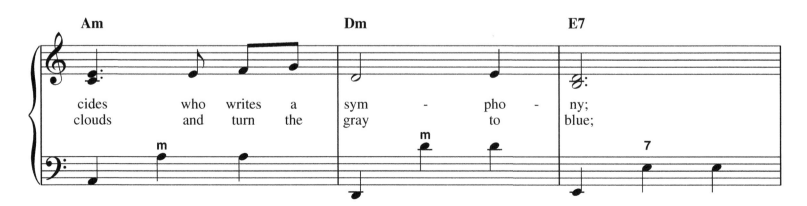

cides who writes a sym - pho - ny;
clouds and turn the gray to blue;

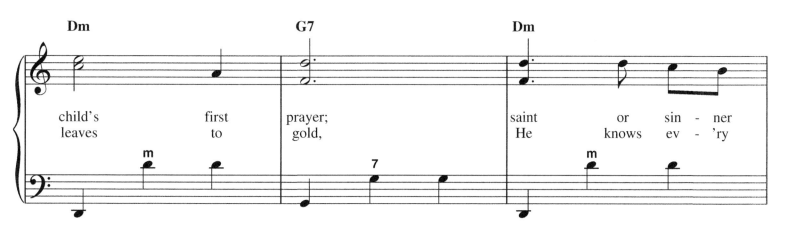

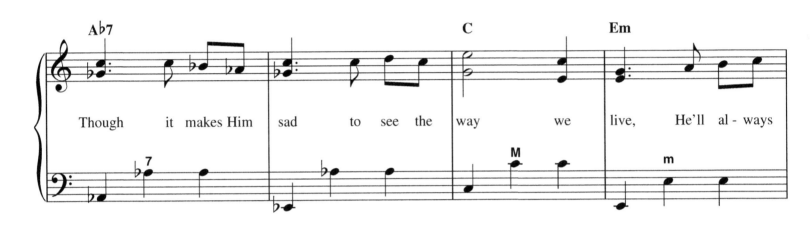

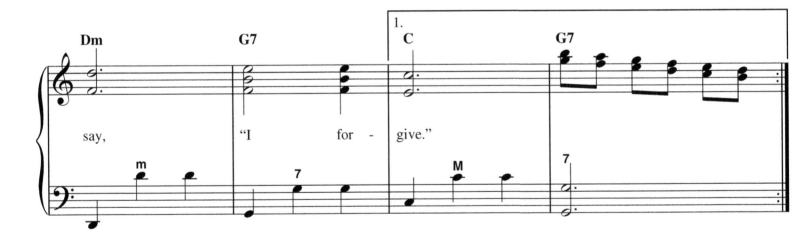

HERE COMES SANTA CLAUS
(Right Down Santa Claus Lane)

Words and Music by GENE AUTRY
and OAKLEY HALDEMAN

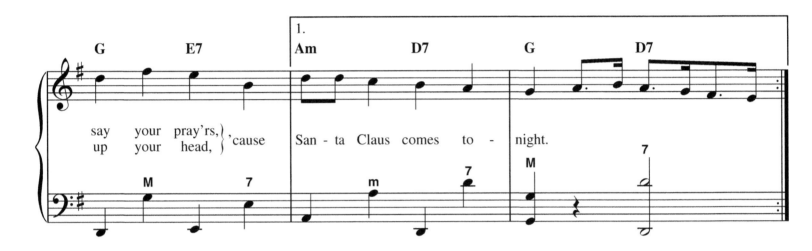

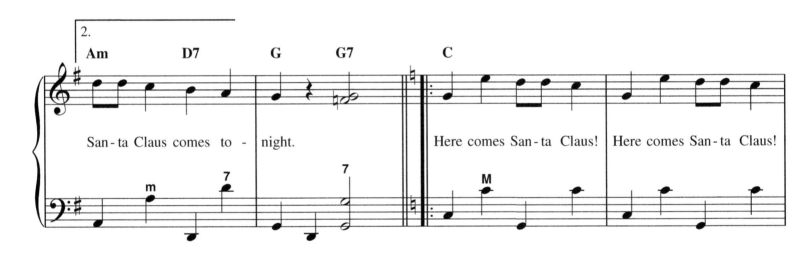

rich or poor for he | loves you just the | same.
chimes ring out; then it's | Christ - mas morn a - | gain.

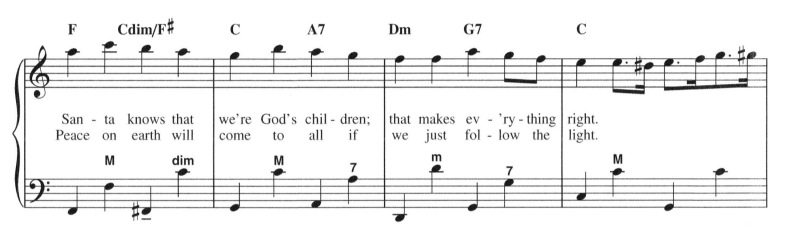

San - ta knows that | we're God's chil - dren; | that makes ev - 'ry - thing | right.
Peace on earth will | come to all if | we just fol - low the | light.

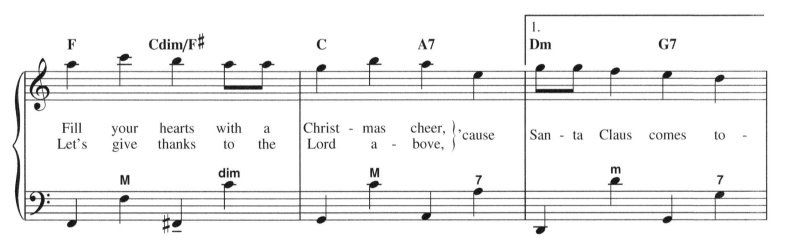

Fill your hearts with a | Christ - mas cheer, } 'cause | San - ta Claus comes to -
Let's give thanks to the | Lord a - bove, }

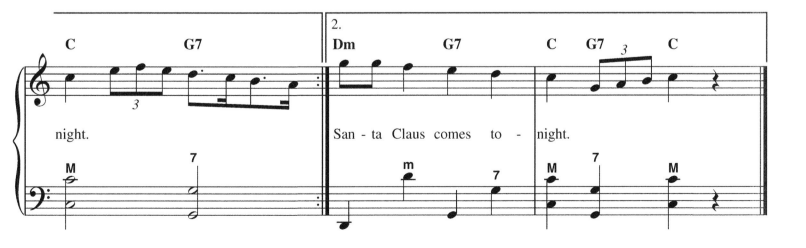

night. | San - ta Claus comes to - | night.

I HEARD THE BELLS ON CHRISTMAS DAY

Words by HENRY WADSWORTH LONGFELLOW
Adapted by JOHNNY MARKS
Music by JOHNNY MARKS

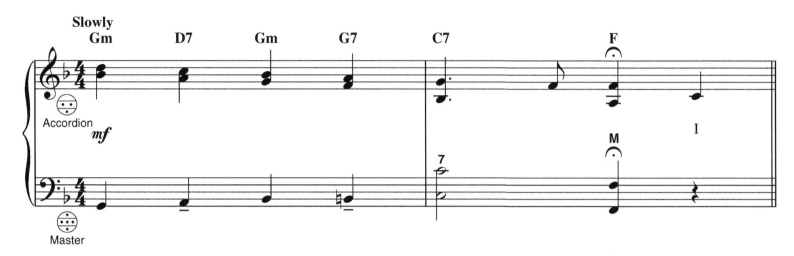

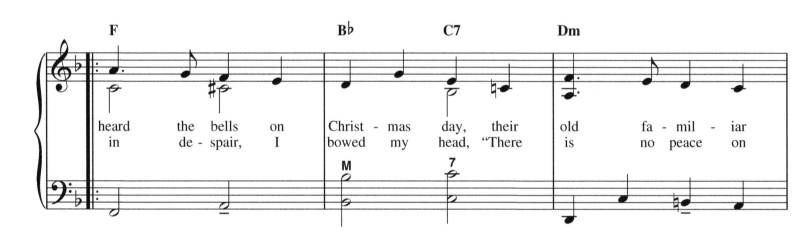

heard the bells on Christ-mas day, their old fa-mil-iar
in de-spair, I bowed my head, "There is no peace on

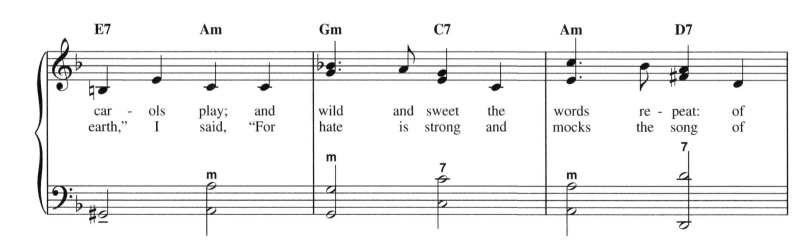

car-ols play; and wild and sweet the words re-peat: of
earth," I said, "For hate is strong and mocks the song of

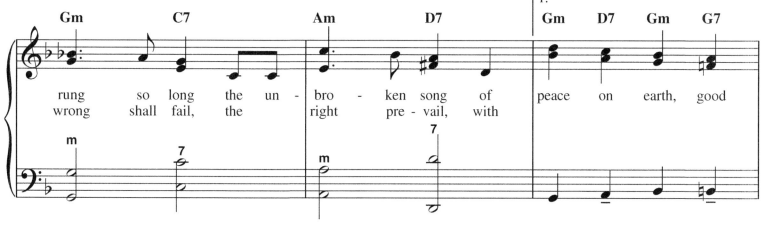

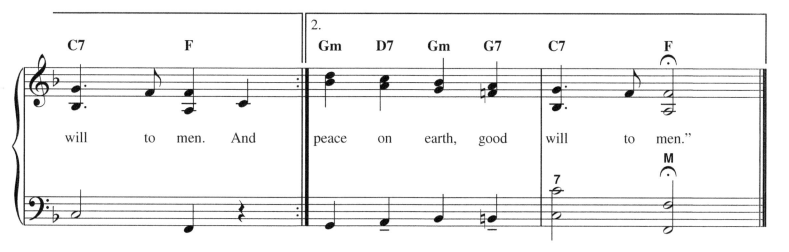

I'VE GOT MY LOVE TO KEEP ME WARM

from the 20th Century Fox Motion Picture ON THE AVENUE

Words and Music by
IRVING BERLIN

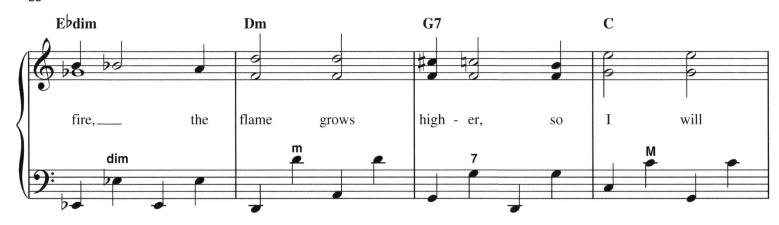

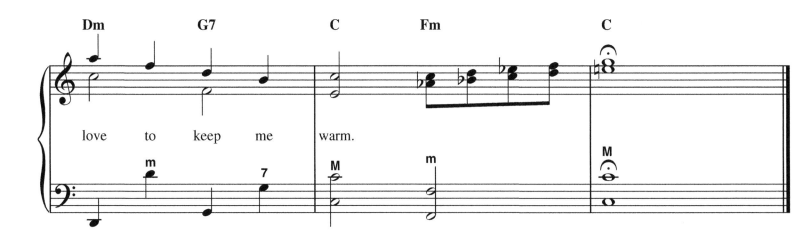

IT'S BEGINNING TO LOOK LIKE CHRISTMAS

By MEREDITH WILLSON

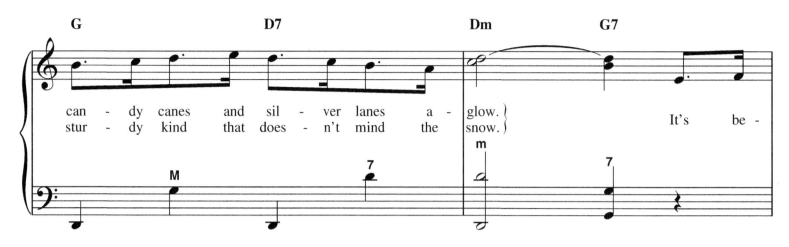

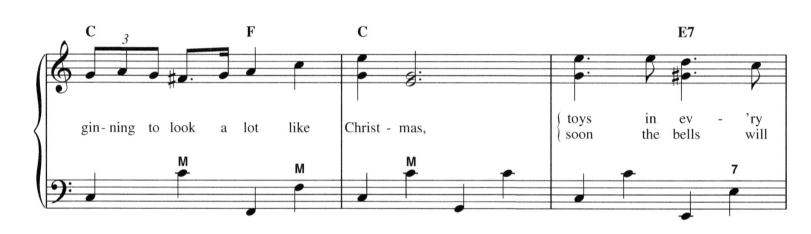

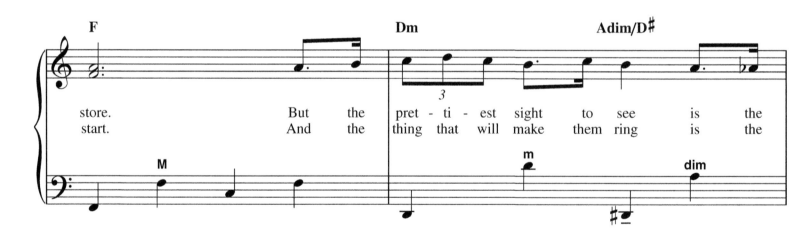

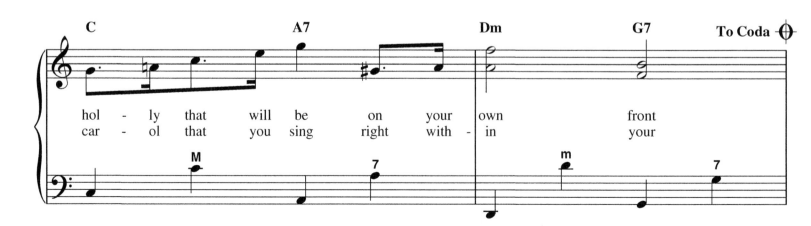

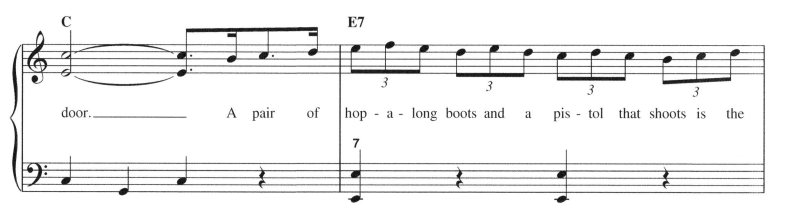

door._____ A pair of hop - a - long boots and a pis - tol that shoots is the

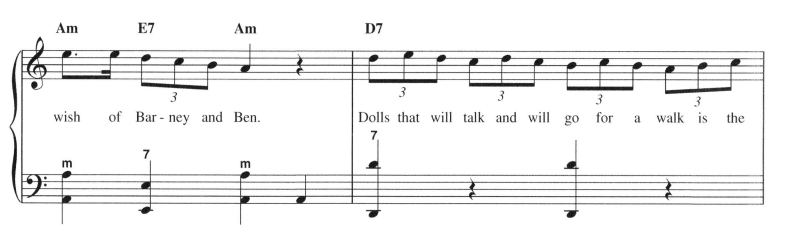

wish of Bar - ney and Ben. Dolls that will talk and will go for a walk is the

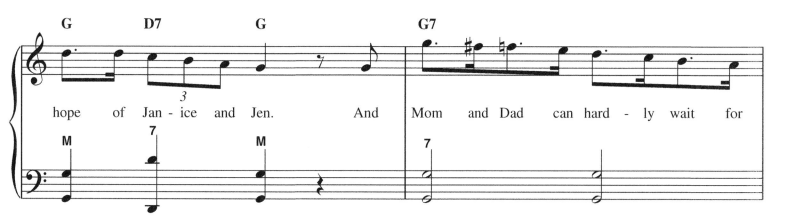

hope of Jan - ice and Jen. And Mom and Dad can hard - ly wait for

school to start a - gain. It's be -

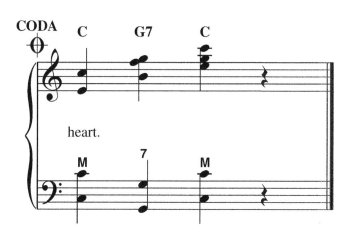

heart.

LET'S HAVE AN OLD FASHIONED CHRISTMAS

Lyric by LARRY CONLEY
Music by JOE SOLOMON

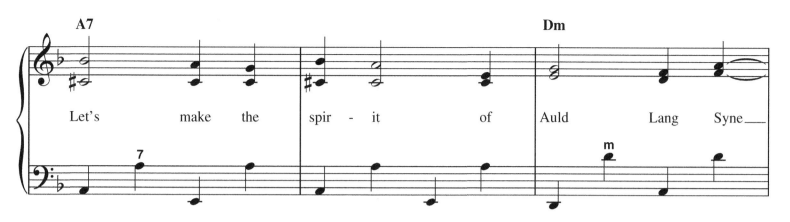

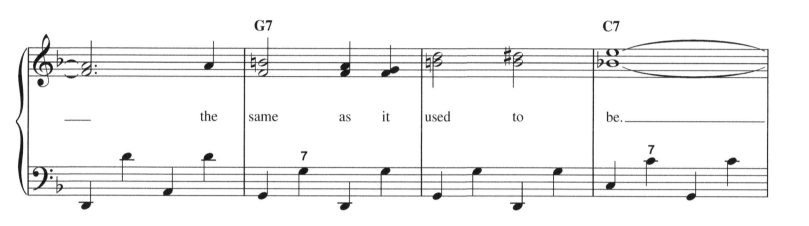

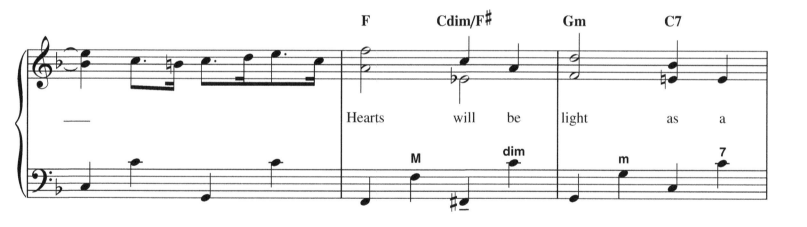

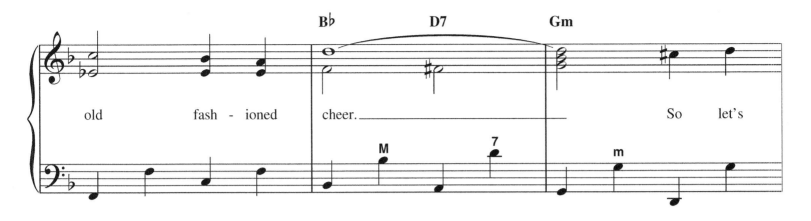

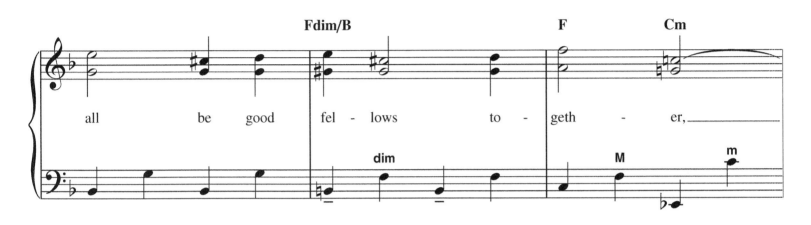

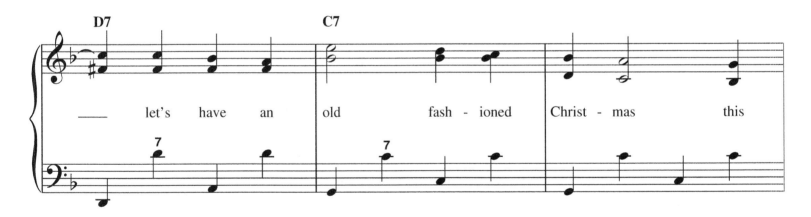

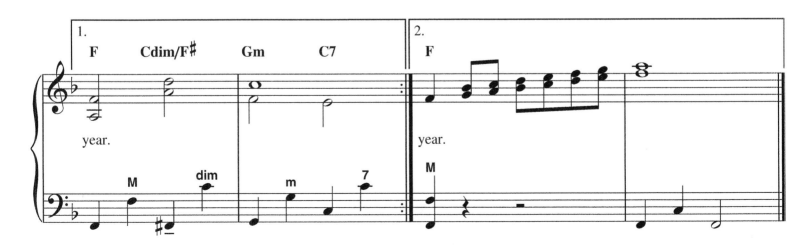

MISTER SANTA

Words and Music by
PAT BALLARD

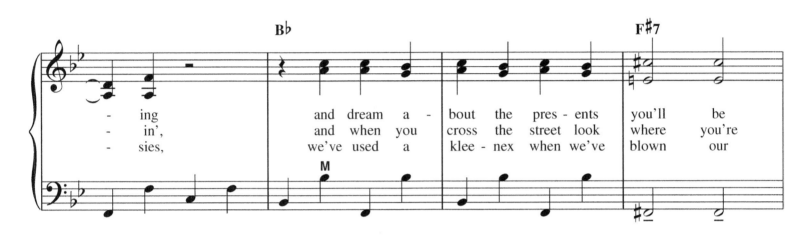

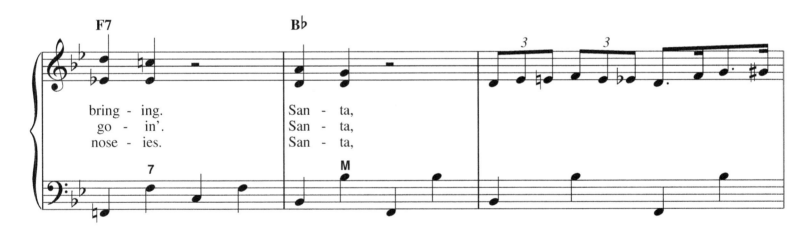

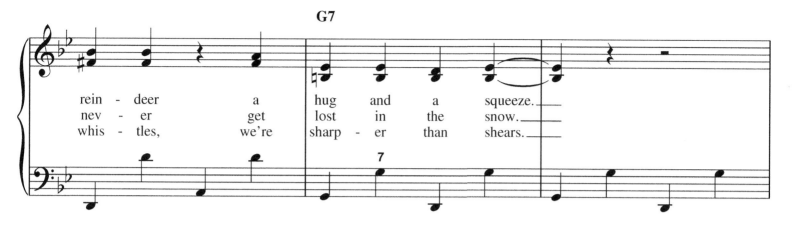

rein - deer a hug and a squeeze.
nev - er get lost in the snow.
whis - tles, we're sharp - er than shears.

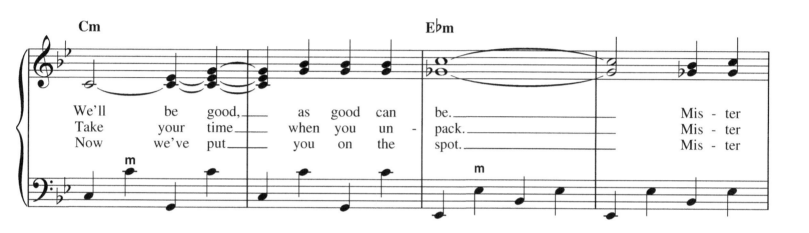

We'll be good, as good can be. Mis - ter
Take your time when you un - pack. Mis - ter
Now we've put you on the spot. Mis - ter

San - ta, don't for - get me.
San - ta, don't hur - ry back.
San - ta, bring us a lot.

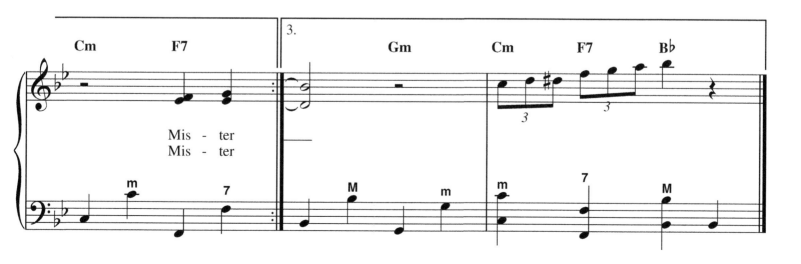

Mis - ter
Mis - ter

MERRY CHRISTMAS, DARLING

Words and Music by RICHARD CARPENTER
and FRANK POOLER

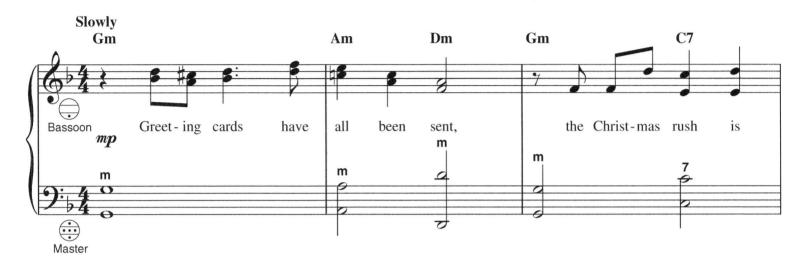

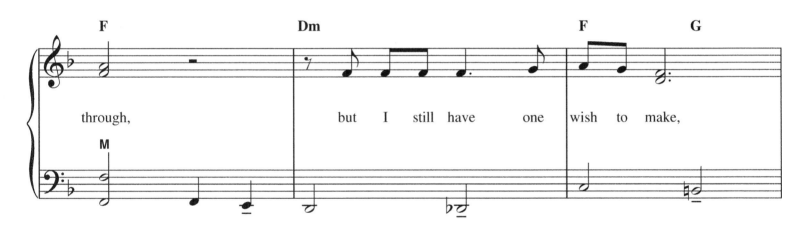

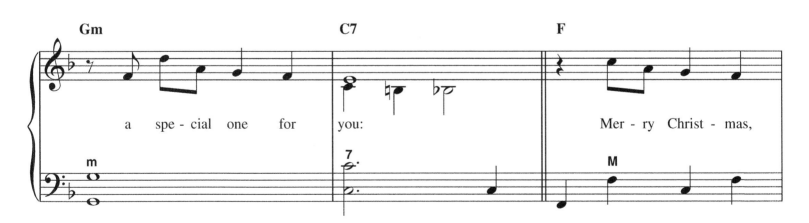

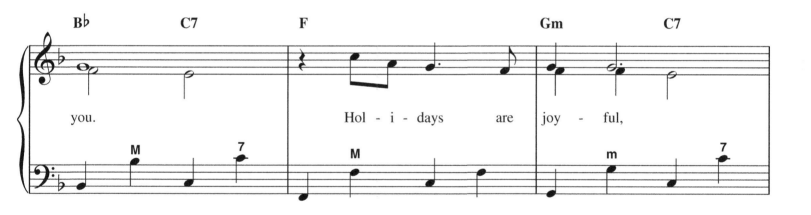

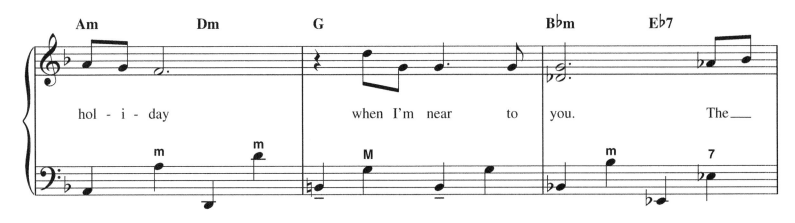

hol - i - day   when I'm near to you.   The ___

lights on my tree I   wish you could see,   I wish it ev - 'ry

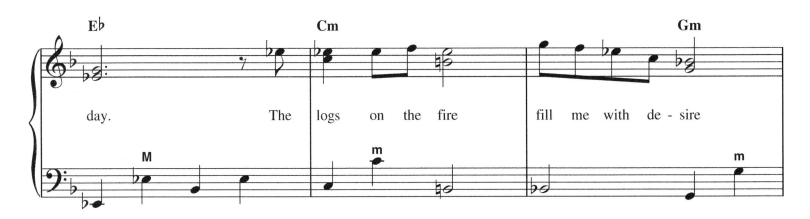

day.   The logs on the fire   fill me with de - sire

to see you and to ___ say   that I wish you mer - ry

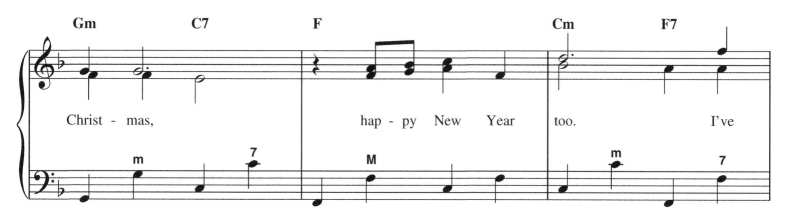

Christ - mas, happy New Year too. I've

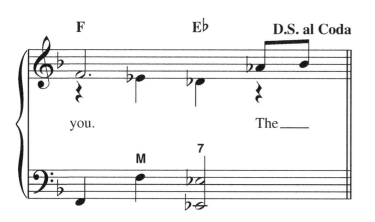

just one wish on this Christ-mas Eve: I wish I were with

To Coda ⊕

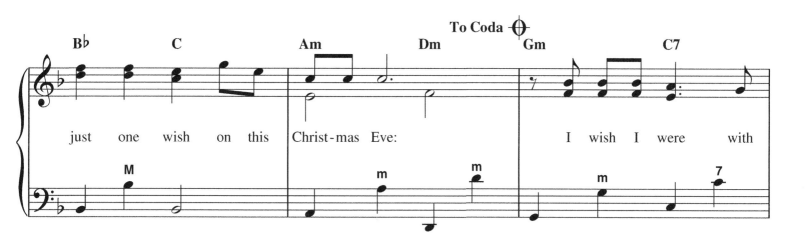

you. The____ I wish I were with

D.S. al Coda   **CODA** ⊕

you, I wish I were with you.

MISTLETOE AND HOLLY

Words and Music by FRANK SINATRA,
DOK STANFORD and HENRY W. SANICOLA

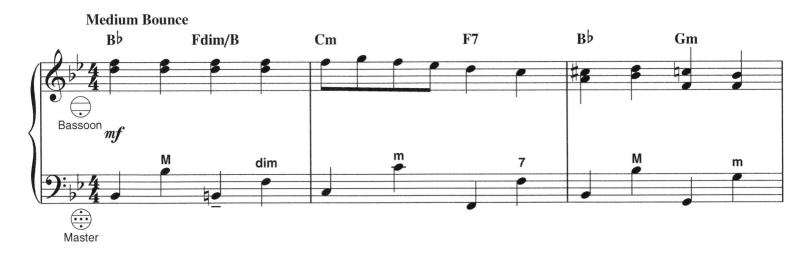

Oh by gosh, by golly, it's time for
Oh by gosh, by jin - gle, it's time for

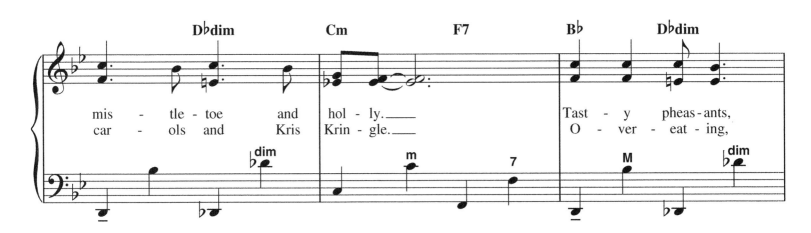

mis - tle - toe and hol - ly.___
car - ols and Kris Krin - gle.___

Tast - y pheas - ants,
O - ver - eat - ing,

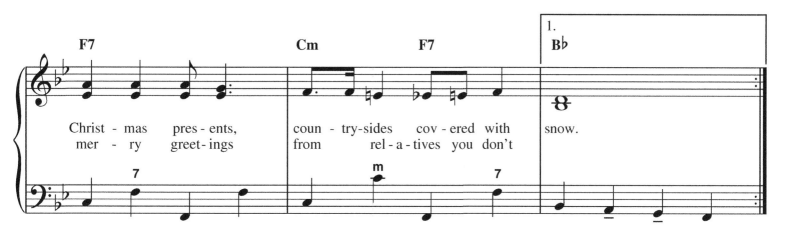

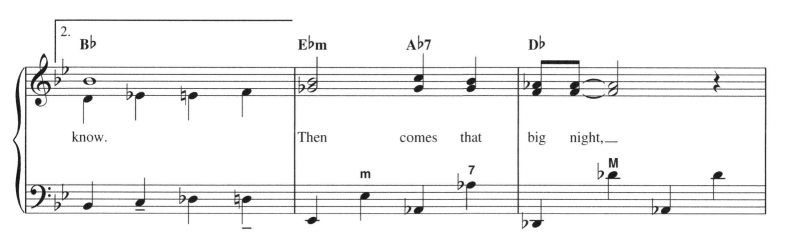

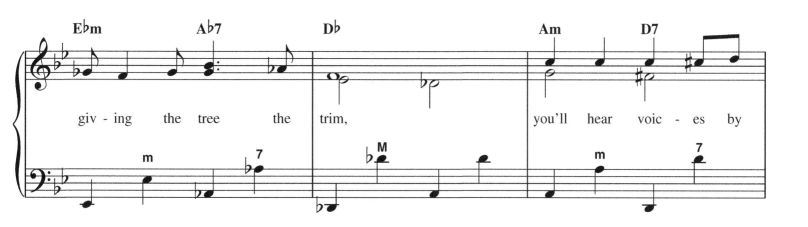

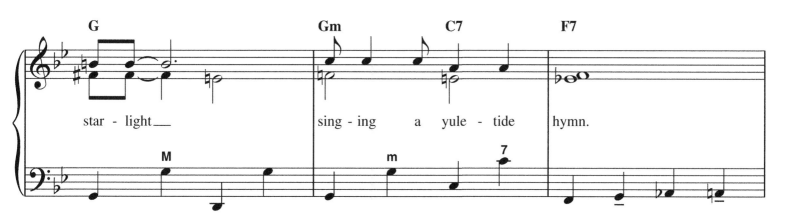

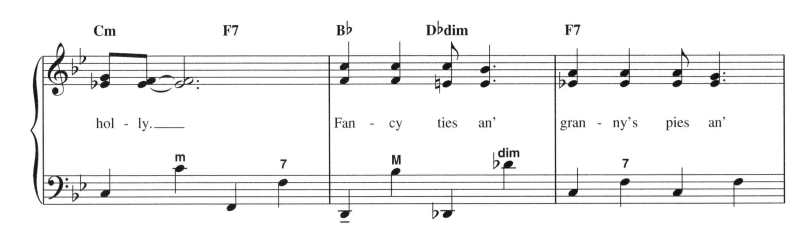

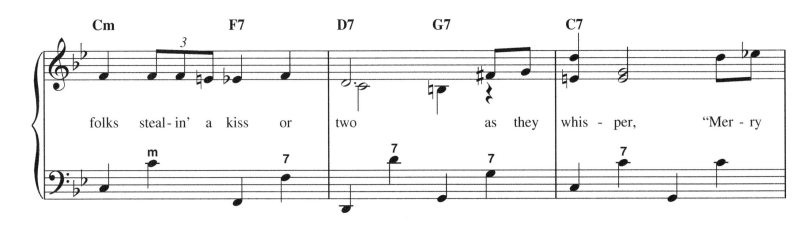

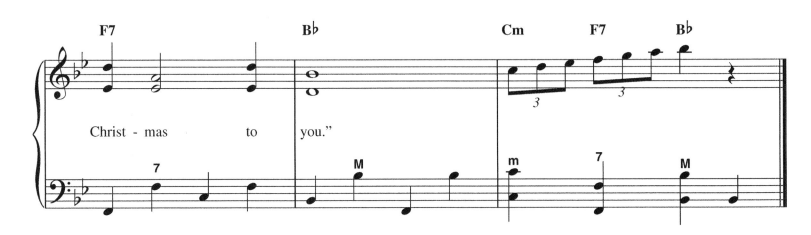

NUTTIN' FOR CHRISTMAS

Words and Music by ROY BENNETT
and SID TEPPER

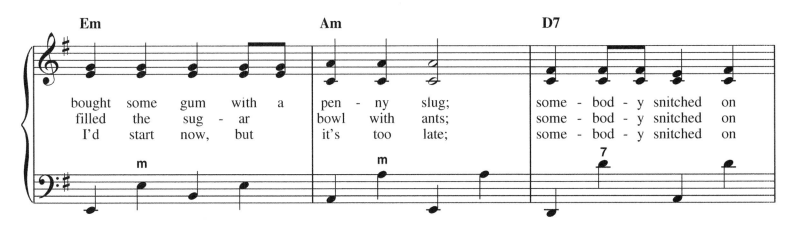

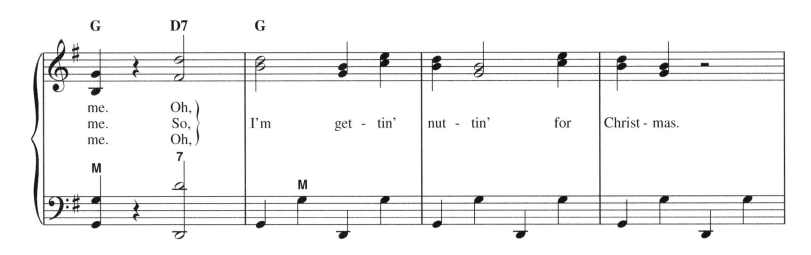

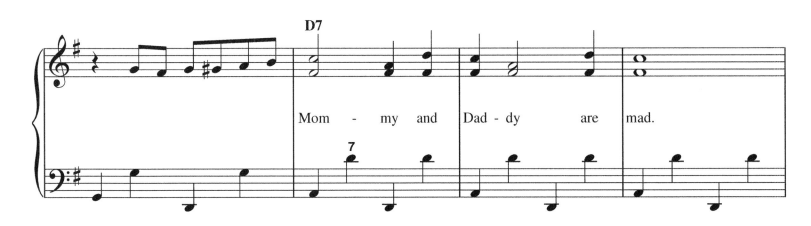

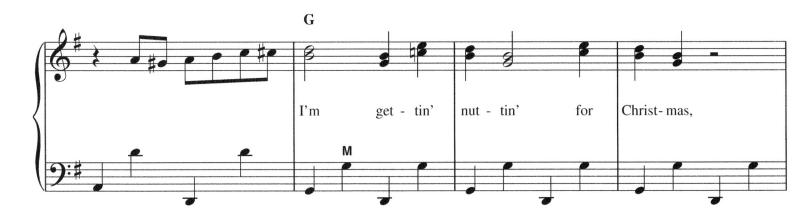

THE MOST WONDERFUL DAY OF THE YEAR

Music and Lyrics by
JOHNNY MARKS

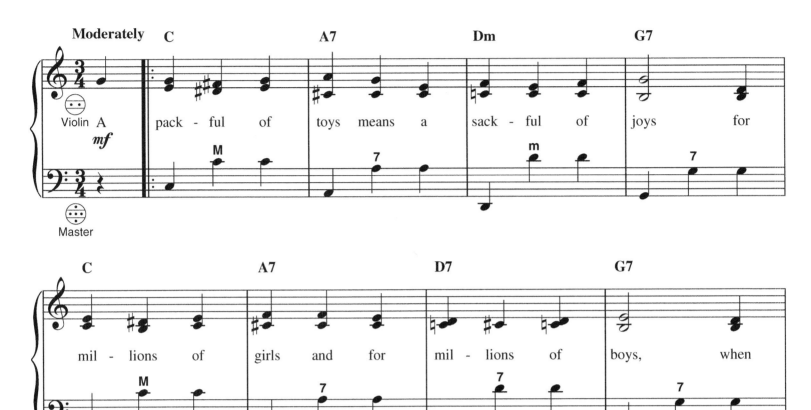

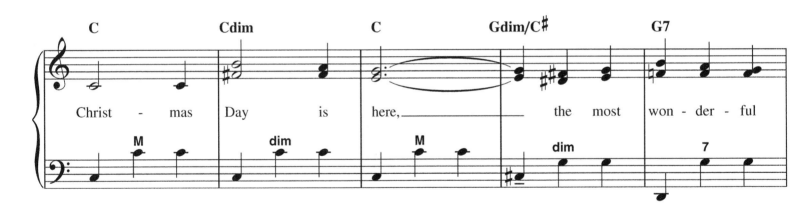

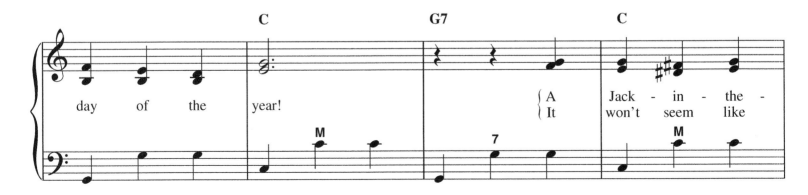

49

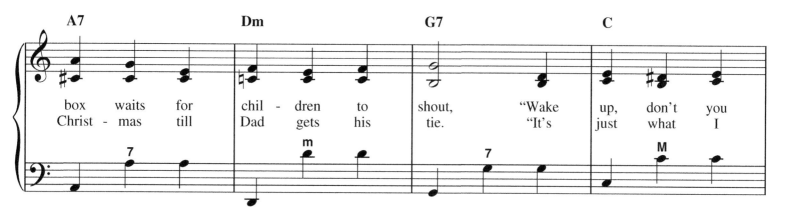

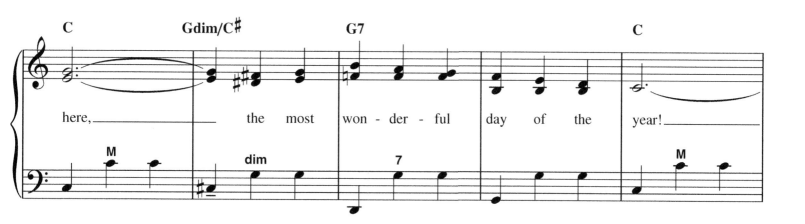

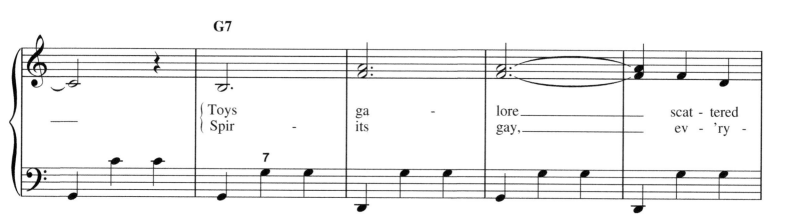

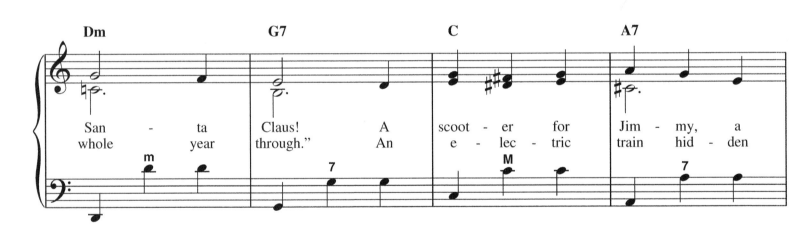

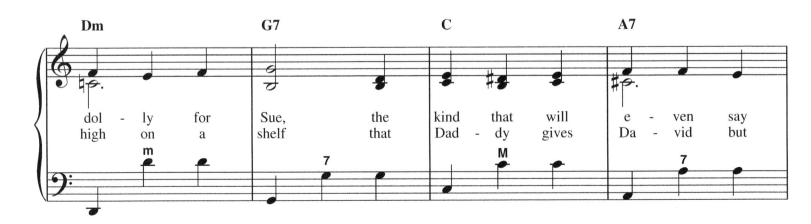

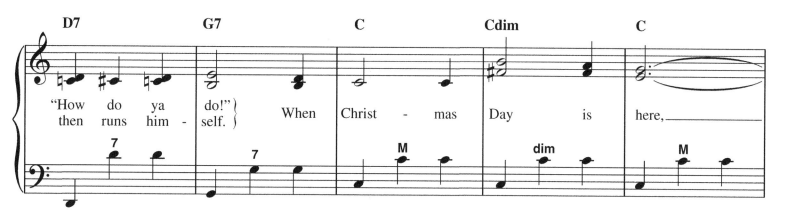

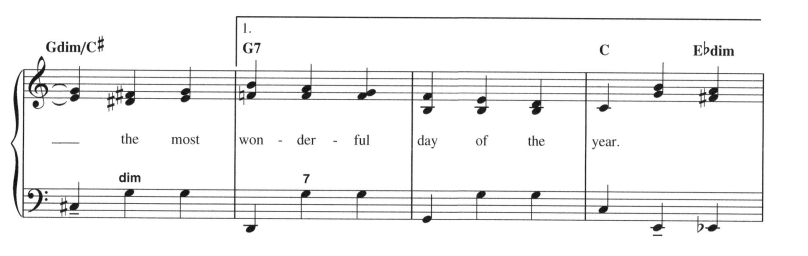

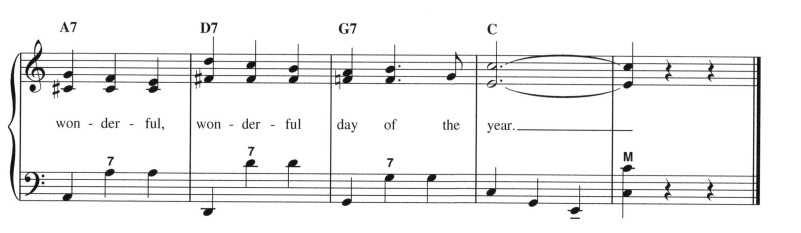

SANTA BABY

By JOAN JAVITS,
PHIL SPRINGER and TONY SPRINGER

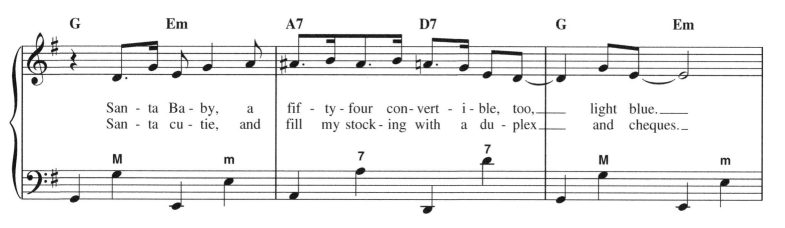

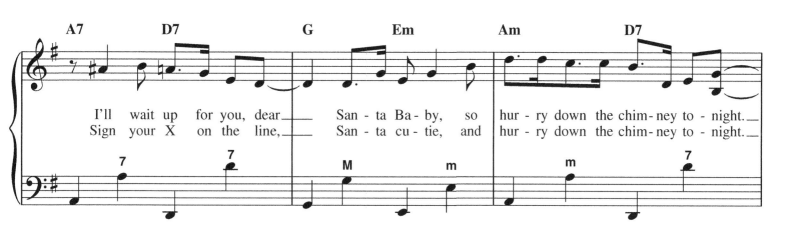

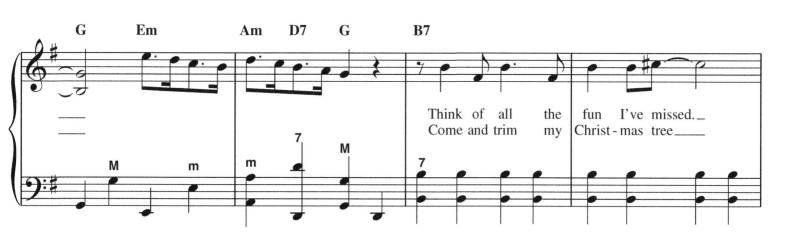

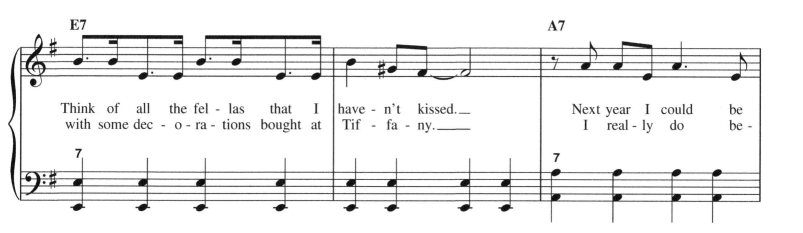

54

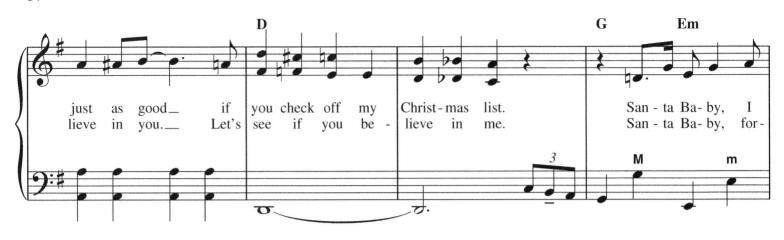

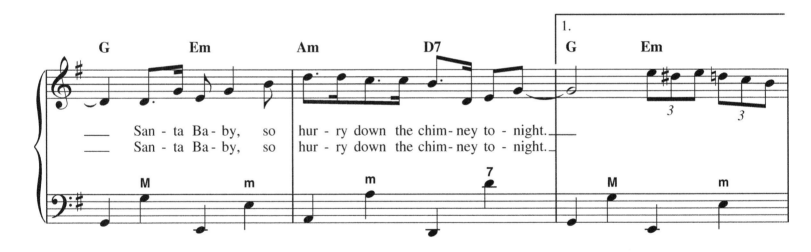

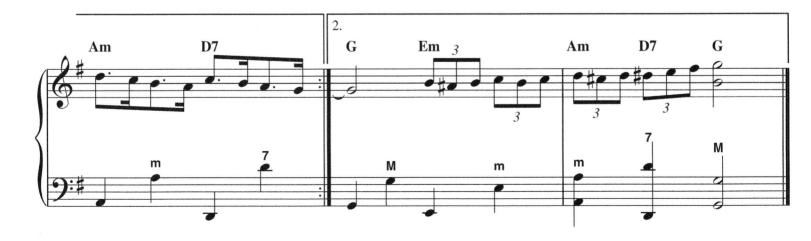

SANTA CLAUS IS COMIN' TO TOWN

Words by HAVEN GILLESPIE
Music by J. FRED COOTS

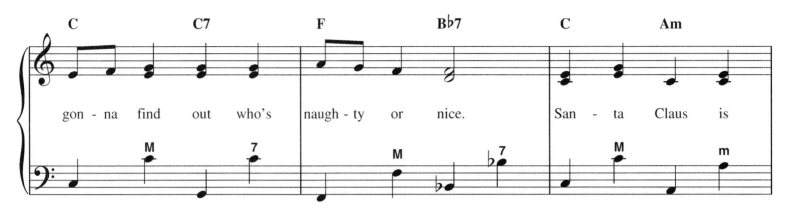

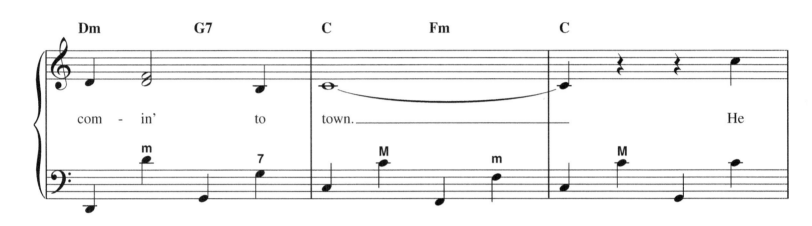

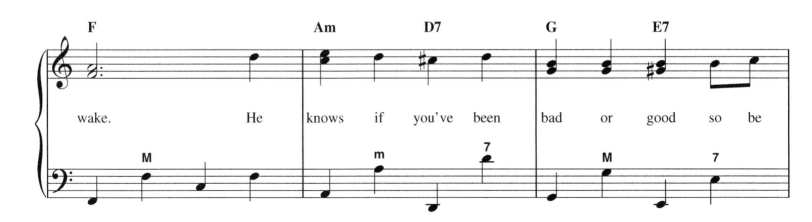

good, for good - ness sake. Oh! You bet - ter watch out, you

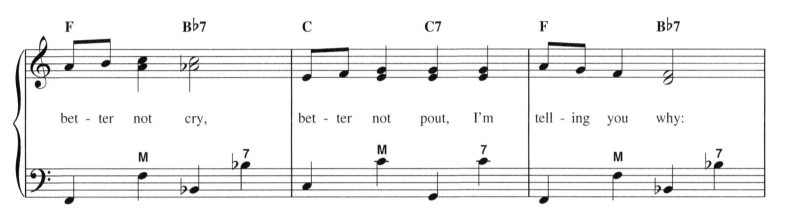

bet - ter not cry, bet - ter not pout, I'm tell - ing you why:

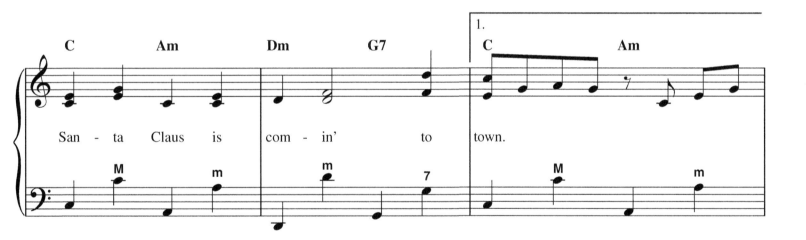

San - ta Claus is com - in' to town.

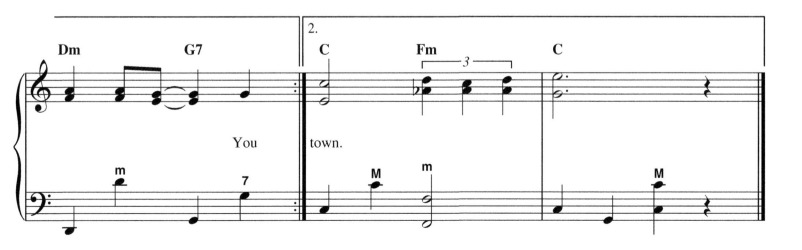

You town.

SILVER AND GOLD

Music and Lyrics by
JOHNNY MARKS

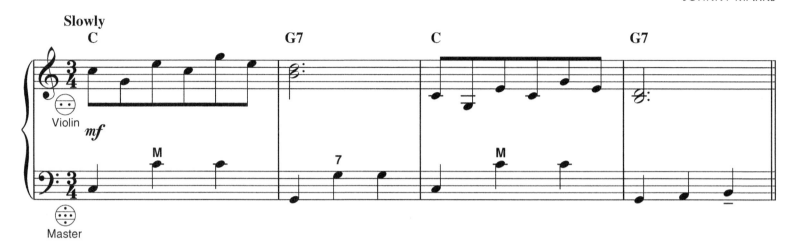

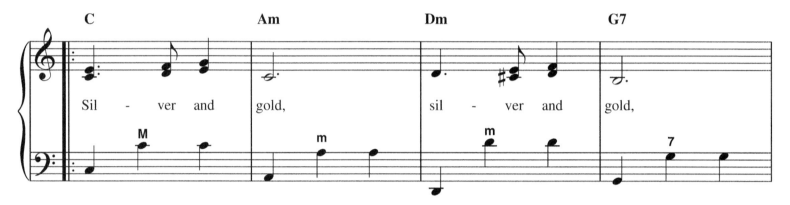

Sil - ver and gold, sil - ver and gold,

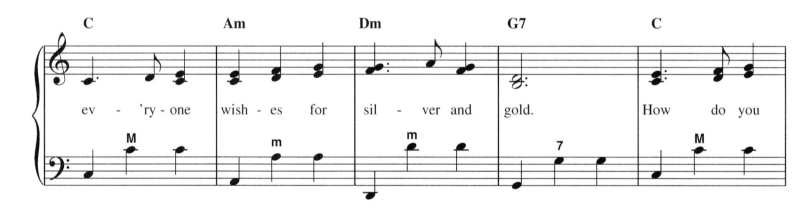

ev - 'ry - one wish - es for sil - ver and gold. How do you

meas - ure its worth? Just by the pleas - ure it

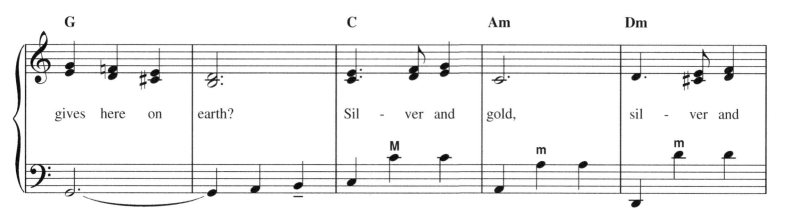

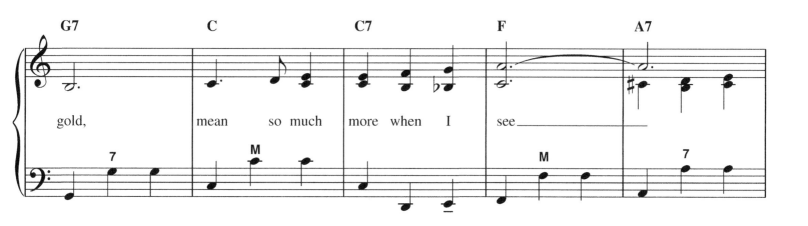

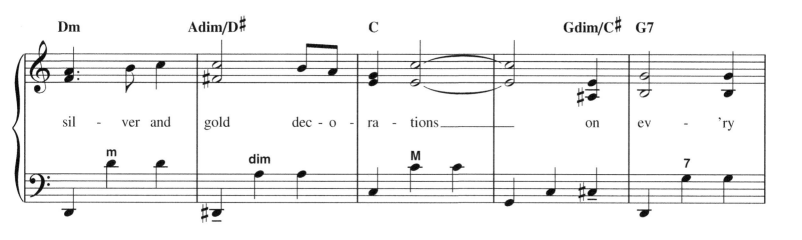

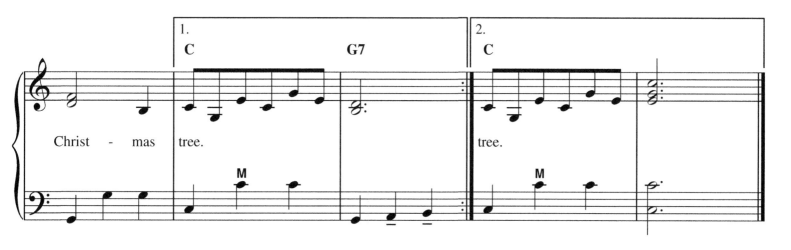

WHAT ARE YOU DOING NEW YEAR'S EVE?

By FRANK LOESSER

Won-der whose arms will hold you good and tight, when it's ex-act-ly

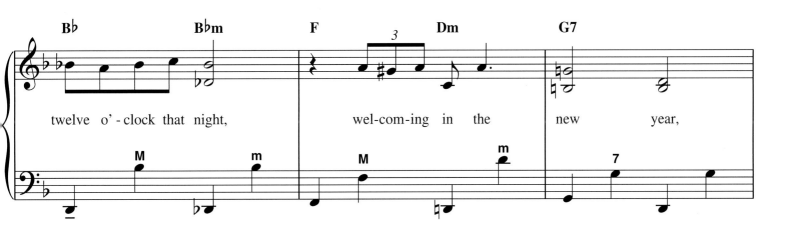

twelve o'-clock that night, wel-com-ing in the new year,

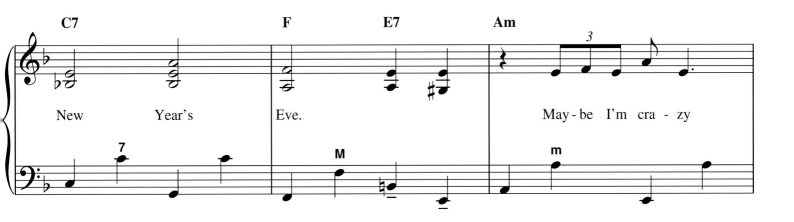

New Year's Eve. May-be I'm cra-zy

to sup-pose I'd ev-er be the one you chose

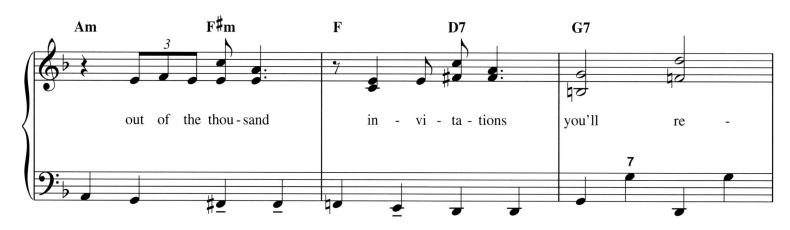

out of the thou - sand   in - vi - ta - tions   you'll   re -

ceive.   Ah, but in case I   stand one lit - tle chance,

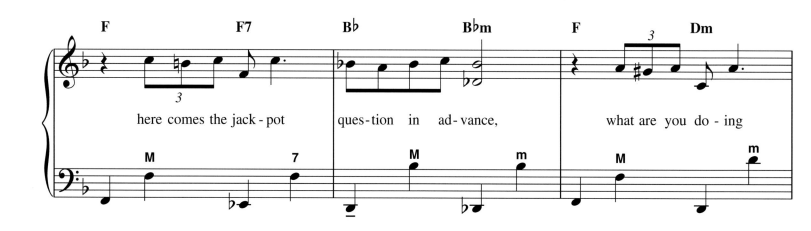

here comes the jack - pot   ques - tion in ad - vance,   what are you do - ing

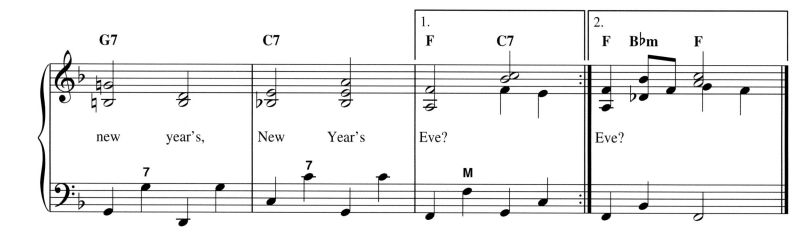

new   year's,   New   Year's   Eve?   Eve?

A COLLECTION OF ALL-TIME FAVORITES
FOR ACCORDION

ACCORDION FAVORITES
arr. Gary Meisner

16 all-time favorites, arranged for accordion, including: Can't Smile Without You • Could I Have This Dance • Endless Love • Memory • Sunrise, Sunset • I.O.U. • and more.
00359012...$12.99

ALL-TIME FAVORITES FOR ACCORDION
arr. Gary Meisner

20 must-know standards arranged for accordions. Includes: Ain't Misbehavin' • Autumn Leaves • Crazy • Hello, Dolly! • Hey, Good Lookin' • Moon River • Speak Softly, Love • Unchained Melody • The Way We Were • Zip-A-Dee-Doo-Dah • and more.
00311088...$12.99

THE BEATLES FOR ACCORDION

17 hits from the Lads from Liverpool have been arranged for accordion. Includes: All You Need Is Love • Eleanor Rigby • The Fool on the Hill • Here Comes the Sun • Hey Jude • In My Life • Let It Be • Ob-La-Di, Ob-La-Da • Penny Lane • When I'm Sixty-Four • Yesterday • and more.
00268724 ....$14.99

BROADWAY FAVORITES
arr. Ken Kotwitz

A collection of 17 wonderful show songs, including: Don't Cry for Me Argentina • Getting to Know You • If I Were a Rich Man • Oklahoma • People Will Say We're in Love • We Kiss in a Shadow.
00490157...$10.99

DISNEY SONGS FOR ACCORDION – 3RD EDITION

13 Disney favorites especially arranged for accordion, including: Be Our Guest • Beauty and the Beast • Can You Feel the Love Tonight • Chim Chim Cher-ee • It's a Small World • Let It Go • Under the Sea • A Whole New World • You'll Be in My Heart • Zip-A-Dee-Doo-Dah • and more!
00152508 ....$12.99

FIRST 50 SONGS YOU SHOULD PLAY ON THE ACCORDION
arr. Gary Meisner

If you're new to the accordion, you are probably eager to learn some songs. This book provides 50 simplified arrangements of must-know popular standards, folk songs and show tunes, including: All of Me • Beer Barrel Polka • Carnival of Venice • Edelweiss • Hava Nagila (Let's Be Happy) • Hernando's Hideaway • Jambalaya (On the Bayou) • Lady of Spain • Moon River • 'O Sole Mio • Sentimental Journey • Somewhere, My Love • That's Amore (That's Love) • Under Paris Skies • and more. Includes lyrics when applicable.
00250269 ....$16.99

FRENCH SONGS FOR ACCORDION
arr. Gary Meisner

A très magnifique collection of 17 French standards arranged for the accordion. Includes: Autumn Leaves • Beyond the Sea • C'est Magnifique • I Love Paris • La Marseillaise • Let It Be Me (Je T'appartiens) • Under Paris Skies • Watch What Happens • and more.
00311498...$10.99

HYMNS FOR ACCORDION
arr. Gary Meisner

24 treasured sacred favorites arranged for accordion, including: Amazing Grace • Beautiful Savior • Come, Thou Fount of Every Blessing • Crown Him with Many Crowns • Holy, Holy, Holy • It Is Well with My Soul • Just a Closer Walk with Thee • A Mighty Fortress Is Our God • Nearer, My God, to Thee • The Old Rugged Cross • Rock of Ages • What a Friend We Have in Jesus • and more.
00277160 ....$9.99

ITALIAN SONGS FOR ACCORDION
arr. Gary Meisner

17 favorite Italian standards arranged for accordion, including: Carnival of Venice • Ciribiribin • Come Back to Sorrento • Funiculi, Funicula • La donna è mobile • La Spagnola • 'O Sole Mio • Santa Lucia • Tarantella • and more.
00311089...$12.99

LATIN FAVORITES FOR ACCORDION
arr. Gary Meisner

20 Latin favorites, including: Bésame Mucho (Kiss Me Much) • The Girl from Ipanema • How Insensitive (Insensatez) • Perfidia • Spanish Eyes • So Nice (Summer Samba) • and more.
00310932...$14.99

THE FRANK MAROCCO ACCORDION SONGBOOK

This songbook includes arrangements and recordings of 15 standards and original songs from legendary jazz accordionist Frank Marocco, including: All the Things You Are • Autumn Leaves • Beyond the Sea • Moon River • Moonlight in Vermont • Stormy Weather (Keeps Rainin' All the Time) • and more!
00233441 Book/Online Audio.............. $19.99

POP STANDARDS FOR ACCORDION
Arrangements of 20 Classic Songs

20 classic pop standards arranged for accordion are included in this collection: Annie's Song • Chances Are • For Once in My Life • Help Me Make It Through the Night • My Cherie Amour • Ramblin' Rose • (Sittin' On) The Dock of the Bay • That's Amore (That's Love) • Unchained Melody • and more.
00254822 ....$14.99

POLKA FAVORITES
arr. Kenny Kotwitz

An exciting new collection of 16 songs, including: Beer Barrel Polka • Liechtensteiner Polka • My Melody of Love • Paloma Blanca • Pennsylvania Polka • Too Fat Polka • and more.
00311573...$12.99

STAR WARS FOR ACCORDION

A dozen songs from the Star Wars franchise: The Imperial March (Darth Vader's Theme) • Luke and Leia • March of the Resistance • Princess Leia's Theme • Rey's Theme • Star Wars (Main Theme) • and more.
00157380 ....$14.99

TANGOS FOR ACCORDION
arr. Gary Meisner

Every accordionist needs to know some tangos! Here are 15 favorites: Amapola (Pretty Little Poppy) • Aquellos Ojos Verdes (Green Eyes) • Hernando's Hideaway • Jalousie (Jealousy) • Kiss of Fire • La Cumparsita (The Masked One) • Quizás, Quizás, Quizás (Perhaps, Perhaps, Perhaps) • The Rain in Spain • Tango of Roses • Whatever Lola Wants (Lola Gets) • and more!
00122252 ....$12.99

3-CHORD SONGS FOR ACCORDION
arr. Gary Meisner

Here are nearly 30 songs that are easy to play but still sound great! Includes: Amazing Grace • Can Can • Danny Boy • For He's a Jolly Good Fellow • He's Got the Whole World in His Hands • Just a Closer Walk with Thee • La Paloma Blanca (The White Dove) • My Country, 'Tis of Thee • Ode to Joy • Oh! Susanna • Yankee Doodle • The Yellow Rose of Texas • and more.
00312104 ....$12.99

LAWRENCE WELK'S POLKA FOLIO

More than 50 famous polkas, schottisches and waltzes arranged for piano and accordion, including: Blue Eyes • Budweiser Polka • Clarinet Polka • Cuckoo Polka • The Dove Polka • Draw One Polka • Gypsy Polka • Helena Polka • International Waltzes • Let's Have Another One • Schnitzelbank • Shuffle Schottische • Squeeze Box Polka • Waldteufel Waltzes • and more.
00123218...$14.99

HAL•LEONARD®
Visit Hal Leonard Online at
www.halleonard.com